Huddled, tired and cold,
we stare into darkness.
The night is long, and danger lurks.
Distant howl, snap of twig.
Something large draws near.

Amber eyes catch the light.
Is it a threat?

No, it is a friend.

The illustrations in this book were made with watercolor and gouache.

Cataloging-in-Publication Data has been applied for and may be obtained from the Library of Congress.

ISBN 978-1-4197-5544-6

Text and illustrations © 2023 Lita Judge
Book design by Heather Kelly

Printed and bound in China
10 9 8 7 6 5 4 3 2

Abrams Books for Young Readers are available at special discounts when purchased in quantity for premiums and promotions as well as fundraising or educational use. Special editions can also be created to specification. For details, contact specialsales@abramsbooks.com or the address below.

Abrams® is a registered trademark of Harry N. Abrams, Inc.

ABRAMS The Art of Books
195 Broadway, New York, NY 10007
abramsbooks.com

For Maia, beloved sight dog and
friend to our aunt, Winnie Judge

DOGS

A History of Our Best Friends

Lita Judge

Abrams Books for Young Readers • New York

Long ago, when humans were still living in caves, wolves were pack-hunting predators with bone-crushing jaws and long, sharp teeth. They could smell prey from a mile away.

Wolves hunted the same herds of caribou, deer, and other large animals as we did. But between 50,000 and 20,000 years ago, something began to change. Wolves and humans became curious toward each other, and some wolves began raising their pups near our encampments. Over time—measured in generations—the physical appearance of these wolves changed. Their snouts and teeth grew shorter.

They had become dogs.

By 19,000 years ago, dogs evolved from a species of gray wolf that is now extinct but once lived in Asia and Europe. They could adapt to living with humans because they already lived in tight-knit social groups and understood working together in packs.

Once they become domesticated—living in a close relationship with humans—all species of animals will vary in appearance from their wild counterparts. In the case of dogs, their tails got curlier, and their ears got floppier than the tails and ears of their wolf ancestors.

They also developed smaller heads, snouts, and teeth as they evolved. One theory for this change is that when animals become less aggressive and have easier access to food, they no longer need such large teeth.

With smaller heads, they had smaller brains. But that didn't mean dogs were less smart.

These early dogs had their own kind of intelligence. They understood the meaning behind some words. And they developed the ability to follow our lead by looking at where we pointed.

Today, chimpanzees and bonobos, our closest relatives, can only look at where we point after intensive training. Dogs can do this without training, even as small puppies.

Dogs even followed our gaze by looking in the same direction as they observed us looking.

Though wolves work together in packs and will follow the gaze of a pack mate, they don't follow the gaze of another species. But if we found something of interest to look at, dogs would look at it, too. No other animal could do that before (or since)! This meant dogs and humans began sharing a silent language that allowed us to work together.

Living with dogs meant that our lives got easier. From far away, we couldn't smell the large animals we hunted. But dogs could.

Dogs have a sense of smell between 10,000 and 100,000 times greater than that of humans.

And we didn't always hear danger approach in the night. But dogs did.

Dogs can hear a wide range of frequencies, including sounds that are four times farther away than humans can hear.

Now we had partners to help us track and hunt, and trusted sentinels to guard our families.

Humans and dogs began relying on each other, and by 15,000 years ago, human cultures all over the world were living alongside dogs.

Our ancestors were hunter-gatherers, constantly on the move in search of food. We couldn't haul heavy loads over long distances. But dogs could.

Several archaeology sites ranging in age from 12,500 to 9,500 years old provide evidence that people living throughout the northern regions of Siberia and the Arctic began using dogsleds for transportation at that time. Sled dogs were physically well suited for the harsh winters and strenuous work. But life was challenging for them, as it was for their human partners. Dogs' and humans' abilities to survive were now linked. Together we could push farther into unknown places in search of food and seek contact with other people and dogs.

Around the same time, in another part of the world, people began domesticating goats and sheep. We couldn't watch our large herds all night and keep them safe from danger. But dogs could.

Raising livestock meant we could give up a hunter-gatherer existence and have a more reliable food source. Some cultures remained nomadic, living in tents and moving their livestock over wide sweeping grasslands with the help of herding dogs. Other cultures began to stay in one place and build villages.

The first livestock were domesticated with the help of herding dogs between 11,000 and 10,000 years ago in the Fertile Crescent, a region of the Middle East.

Fossil evidence can tell us much about what ancient dogs looked like, but we can only guess at their fur length and color. The earliest art left by humans depicting dogs doesn't appear until about 9,000 years ago.

Whether people were nomadic or lived in permanent settlements, our dogs had gone from life on the edge of our encampments to trusted family members in our homes. We grew attached to them, gave them names, and in many cases, when they died, gave them ceremonial burials.

Several burial sites for dogs dating as far back as 12,000 years have been found in the Middle East, Siberia, East Asia, and Europe.

Within an Egyptian tomb, a stone tablet with hieroglyphics dating from 2650 BCE gives us the first record of a dog's name: Abuwtiyuw. The tablet also tells us that this beloved dog spent his life guarding the Pharaoh. Upon Abuwtiyuw's death, he was mummified and laid to rest within a tomb built especially for him. Other texts tell us the Egyptians shaved all their hair when their dogs died. They only shaved their eyebrows when the family's cat died.

BRAVE ONE

RELIABLE

YELP

Inscribed dog collars and texts tell us other names the ancient Egyptians, Greeks, and Romans gave their dogs. When you translate the names into English, it's not hard to imagine something about their personality, or what roles these canine companions may have performed.

TRACKER

USELESS

GOOD HERDSMAN

Most dogs who lived within homes had to work alongside their human companions. But a few lucky pups, especially small dogs, lived in the lap of luxury.

In the first century BCE, Chinese royals began favoring small dogs for pets. The rage for dogs who could comfortably sit on their human's lap or in the sleeves of robes quickly spread to Japan and other parts of Asia.

By the Middle Ages, European nobility considered it the height of fashion to carry a small ribbon-adorned dog. Henry III of France carried his fluffy favorite in a basket tied around his neck.

This rage continued through the centuries amongst anyone who could afford to keep a pet dog. The relationship between humans and their devoted "lap warmers" may have started as a symbol of wealth and status—but the loving bond was real.

In the Middle Ages, without the advantages of modern medicine, doctors could do little to heal their patients. But dogs could help.

Healers couldn't see hidden diseases, like cancer. But they found that dogs, with their keen sense of smell, could.

And though doctors didn't understand why, many found that patients suffering from serious injuries had a better chance of surviving if a dog licked their wounds. Much later, scientists learned that a dog's saliva contains a chemical that helps prevent infection.

By the sixteenth century, doctors began prescribing dogs for treatments. If you suffered from an upset stomach, you should hold a small dog to your chest!

Doctors at the time had no way of knowing why this treatment worked. But we now know that when we pet a dog, our blood pressure and cortisol (the stress hormone) levels are lowered. That means we feel less anxiety. No wonder a dog can help relieve symptoms of a stomachache brought on by stress.

Dogs performed many other tasks that we couldn't do alone. We couldn't swim for long in icy water to retrieve a duck for dinner. But dogs could.

Dogs who were strong swimmers and resilient to cold water, like poodles, were trained to accompany hunters and retrieve game birds from lakes.

Some, like the Portuguese water dog, even worked on fishing boats, herding fish into nets and retrieving tackle. Most retrievers were highly trained and generally well cared for.

Farmers couldn't find tasty
truffles to eat. But dogs could.

*Lagotti Romagnoli have a keen sense of smell and have
helped European truffle farmers since the Middle Ages find
hidden truffles, a mushroom-like fungus that grows below
the surface of the soil and is highly valued as a food delicacy.*

Dogs even
helped us cook.

*Starting in sixteenth-century
England, turnspit dogs ran
in treadmill wheels like giant
hamsters to rotate meat over
our hearths, churn butter, or
grind grain. Unfortunately,
these dogs endured long days
filled with strenuous work.*

And if dinner ignited into flames, dogs helped us put out the fire!

Firehouses in the United States and Europe throughout the eighteenth and nineteenth centuries adopted dalmatians for their calming influence with skittish carriage horses. When an alarm sounded, the dalmatians ran out of the firehouse, barking to clear a path in crowded streets for the fire wagon. The dogs then ran alongside the horses to keep them from spooking as they neared panicked people and flames.

For centuries, different types of dogs were grouped into breeds, which were defined by the functions they performed. For example, sheepdogs herded flocks, running hounds helped hunters, and mastiffs were guard dogs.

Then, in 1859, Victorians in England held the first dog show. More shows soon followed and soared in popularity. From then on, people began grouping dogs by their physical appearance, and dog breeds were defined by how dogs looked.

Early dog shows were like beauty contests for pooches. Caught up in the obsession, people wanted dogs to be smaller, or taller, or to have unusual coats. Some even bred dogs to have bigger eyes and smaller snouts so that they looked more like puppies when grown. By choosing which dogs they bred together, people created new dog breeds.

SCOTTISH TERRIER + MALTESE = YORKSHIRE TERRIER

Suddenly there were more dog breeds than ever before.

The majority of modern dog breeds originated within a fifty-year span of the Victorian era. Sadly, there have been some harmful outcomes to dogs. By artificially controlling how dogs look on the outside, we have neglected their health on the inside. The result is that many dogs have serious health problems.

Ever since dogs were domesticated, their fate has been tied to ours—even if, unfortunately, that means serving in wars.

In 1914, World War I broke out. It involved over 100 countries, and more dogs served in militaries than ever before. For the first time, dogs were highly trained in military dog schools to perform a wide range of life-saving tasks. People were reminded that it didn't matter how our dogs looked—we needed their help.

Throughout ancient history, the Egyptians, Greeks, Persians, Sarmatians, Baganda, Slavs, Britons, and Romans all had dogs who served as sentries or went into battle. But with advanced training methods during WWI, dogs were trusted to carry vital messages attached to their collars when all other forms of communication were down. They also warned soldiers of approaching danger, hauled supplies, and detected explosives. Red Cross and Mercy dogs located wounded soldiers and carried first aid kits to them. Some even pulled injured soldiers to safety on two-wheeled carts. Though dogs don't sign up for war, many were heroes. Some were awarded medals; sadly, thousands gave their lives.

After peace was declared, countless soldiers returned home from WWI forever changed. Thousands had been injured in gas attacks and faced difficult lives because they could no longer see. But dogs trained as sight dogs were smart enough to see for them.

As far back as the first century AD, a blind person being led by a dog on a leash is depicted on a Roman mural. Over the centuries, there have been many examples throughout Europe and Asia of dogs helping the blind. But the first schools devoted to training sight dogs opened in Germany following WWI to meet the crushing need. Programs throughout Europe, the United States, and elsewhere soon followed, to help all blind people live more independent lives.

Sight dogs were so effective at helping people that programs to train new kinds of service dogs followed. Now there are dogs to assist people who are deaf, living with epilepsy, or facing other physical disabilities.

The most common are therapy dogs, who bring comfort to people in nursing homes and hospitals or live with people suffering with emotional distress.

Today, dogs live in partnership with us in more ways than ever before.

Military dogs work in war zones to find explosives.

Dogs are elite athletes.

Dogs are world-record holders and entertainers.

Hotel worker dogs detect bedbugs.

Search and rescue dogs help find lost people.

RESCUE

Dogs clear birds from airport runways during takeoff.

And of course, many dogs are just face-licking, sandwich-snatching family members.

Scent dogs help identify COVID-19 in airports and other crowded public places.

Police dogs help solve crimes.

Anyone whose family includes a dog knows what a wondrous thing it is to come home to excited tail wags and face licks. You know that you love your dog. And you know they missed you while you were away. But does your dog love you back?

If you have a dog, you are probably nodding your head. Science has proven you are right.

Scientists believe dogs can empathize with us, meaning they experience negative emotions when they see their human suffer. And they communicate with us through facial expressions, body gestures, barks, whimpers, and tail wags. But to answer the question of whether they love us, we have to look deeper.

Hormones in their blood tell us how they feel. Just as we experience lower blood pressure and cortisol levels when we pet a dog, they experience the same benefit. That means we aren't the only ones to feel more relaxed from our bond—dogs feel it, too.

Perhaps even more amazingly, when humans and dogs stare into each other's eyes, both of our brains release a hormone called oxytocin! This "hugging hormone" is the same hormone mothers produce when they hold their babies and experience feelings of love, maternal bonding, and protectiveness.

Dogs and humans are connected.

For thousands of years, we have benefited from our relationship with dogs. They have comforted us, carried us, worked for us, and saved our lives. In almost every way imaginable, they have cared for us.

Dogs need a safe home, food, and care in return.
But perhaps the most important thing dogs and
humans can share is . . .

ANIMAL SHELTER

ADOPT A
SHELTER PET

. . . love.

AUTHOR'S NOTE

I spent much of my childhood living in remote places. Everyone loved animals in my family, and we had a variety of cats, birds, small rodents, a lizard, even a raccoon, and an owl that we nursed back to health. But the reason my mom felt it was safe for me to explore the woods alone was because of our dog, Keyair. He was a curly-haired Chesapeake Bay retriever, bigger than me for several years. The first word I learned was "Sit," and Keyair sat at my command for six months before deciding that protecting me from harm was far more important. Keyair guarded me like a mother bear when my parents were out of sight. And he curled up next to me at night to make sure I stayed warm.

So many of us have a strong attachment to a beloved family dog. And if we don't personally love a dog, we probably know someone who does. Of all the animals on the planet, they serve the widest range of roles in our lives, from companions to protectors, helpers, and lifesavers. As they have done throughout history, they continue to help us with tasks, some of which may not be possible without them. Over and over, they have proven themselves to be loyal and even understanding. It's no wonder a phrase that described their relationship with us as "man's best friend"—first used by Frederick the Great of Prussia in the 1700s—is still used today. Though it has been updated, rightly, to "man's *and woman's* best friend"!

Dogs are embedded in our culture. They have been symbols of wealth, status, and loyalty; subjects of our myths and folklore; and even worshipped as gods by some ancient cultures. Today, dogs all over the world keep up with the times, gaining millions of followers on Instagram and TikTok (with the help of their humans, of course!). Most of us have enjoyed the antics and personality of at least one dog with celebrity status.

But not all dogs are pets. There are an estimated 900 million dogs alive today worldwide. Between 17 and 24 percent of them live as pets or working dogs, while most of the remaining dogs, around 700 million, are feral, meaning they are free-roaming. Like their ancient ancestors, these dogs are less socialized to humans, but they still rely on our settlements, finding food by scavenging on trash. They are unlike stray dogs, who once lived as companions but then became homeless; feral dogs have never lived as human companions. Most live in areas of warmer climates within India, Southeast Asia, Africa, Mexico, and South America.

The author with her dog, Keyair

Unfortunately, like many animals, some dogs who live as companions to humans are treated unkindly. And millions of dogs in the United States alone are cast off annually to animal shelters and are in need of homes. Rescue organizations like the American Society for the Prevention of Cruelty to Animals (ASPCA) and the Humane Society of the United States work tirelessly to safeguard the welfare of all dogs. Many other organizations that protect the welfare of animals have been established worldwide.

There is much we can do to help dogs:

- Support nonprofit organizations that work to rescue animals from abuse and neglect by either volunteering or donating to fundraising efforts.

- If you have a dog, provide them with a collar and identification tag, or consider having your veterinarian implant a microchip so that your dog can be identified if lost.

- If you see a dog running loose, call your local police or humane society to ensure that a family dog can be reunited with their human, or a stray dog can be sheltered and put up for adoption.

- If you are planning on bringing a dog into your family, consider adopting from a rescue shelter.

- If you do select a dog from a breeder, interview them carefully to ensure they are providing healthy conditions for dog parents and puppies.

- When adopting a dog, consult a veterinarian to find which breeds are healthy. Also make a thoughtful choice about what kind of dog to get. Different breeds vary greatly in temperament. Some are calm and gentle, while others are high-energy and need to live active lives. Choose a dog whose lifestyle is compatible with your own.

- Once you have a dog, attend dog training classes together. Dogs are intelligent and naturally inclined to live cooperatively with us, but first we must learn how to communicate clearly with them.

DOG BREEDS

Today there are nearly 400 dog breeds recognized all over the world, from a pocket-sized Chihuahua weighing about one pound to a record-breaking 343-pound English mastiff. Dogs vary in appearance more than any other animal species on the planet. Turn the page for just a few.

DOG BREEDS

DOBERMAN PINSCHER

GREYHOUND

GERMAN SHEPHERD

AFGHAN HOUND

KOMONDOR

IRISH SETTER

GOLDEN RETRIEVER

STANDARD POODLE

SIBERIAN HUSKY

BORDER COLLIE

BICHON FRISE

POMERANIAN

JACK RUSSELL TERRIER

SHIH TZU

SCOTTISH TERRIER

PUG

CHINESE CRESTED

IRISH WOLFHOUND

GREAT DANE

ENGLISH MASTIFF

TIBETAN MASTIFF

ENGLISH BULLDOG

BASSET HOUND

BEAGLE

ENGLISH SPRINGER
SPANIEL

LABRADOODLE

WIRE FOX
TERRIER

PEMBROKE WELSH CORGI

PAPILLON

PEKINGESE

YORKSHIRE TERRIER

CHIHUAHUA

DACHSHUND

MALTESE

FAMOUS DOGS

Most people can name at least one famous dog, whether from watching TV or movies, following social media, or reading books. Here are a few of my favorites.

During the fourteenth century, a religious pilgrim named Roche suffered from the bubonic plague. He lay waiting to die, but his dog saved his life by bringing him bread and licking his plague sores. Roche became known as the patron saint of dogs in the Catholic faith. Perhaps his dog should have been sainted, too.

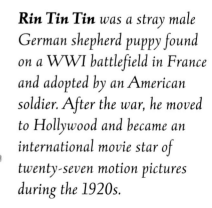

*In 1903 a pit bull terrier named **Bud Nelson** captured newspaper headlines, as he and his human companions, Horatio Nelson Jackson and Sewall K. Crocker, became the first to cross the United States in the newly invented automobile. The goggles Bud wore to protect his eyes from dust in the roofless car remain on display at the Smithsonian Museum of American History.*

*A bull terrier named **Sergeant Stubby** served during WWI and was honored with many medals of valor for saving the lives of American soldiers. Upon his death, he received a fifteen-paragraph obituary in the New York Times.*

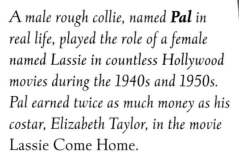

***Rin Tin Tin** was a stray male German shepherd puppy found on a WWI battlefield in France and adopted by an American soldier. After the war, he moved to Hollywood and became an international movie star of twenty-seven motion pictures during the 1920s.*

*A male rough collie, named **Pal** in real life, played the role of a female named Lassie in countless Hollywood movies during the 1940s and 1950s. Pal earned twice as much money as his costar, Elizabeth Taylor, in the movie Lassie Come Home.*

In 1950, Charles M. Schulz's black-and-white dog, **Spike,** inspired the character Snoopy, who appears in the comic strip Peanuts. This quiet but strong-willed canine remains a beloved icon of American pop culture.

In 2019, a border collie named **Chaser** could identify and retrieve 1,022 objects by name. She had the largest tested memory of any nonhuman animal.

Bretagne, a golden retriever, was one of about 300 search dogs to help firefighters find survivors and human remains after the September 11, 2001, terrorist attacks in New York City. She went on to serve during Hurricanes Katrina and Ivan. Bretagne lived a long life and was believed to be the last surviving search and rescue dog from 9/11. Firefighters and first responders lined the sidewalk to salute this heroic dog upon her death in 2016.

A blue heeler/Catahoula mix named **Stella** was the first dog to speak by pushing buttons on a soundboard originally designed to help nonverbal people communicate. With the help of her human, Christina Hunger, she has learned to put simple phrases of up to five words together. She can say "all done want bed" when she is tired. She can also request "all done bed come outside," "walk park now," "help ball" when her toy is out of reach, and "love you." Stella is still learning new phrases and has inspired other dogs and humans to communicate this way.

Jiffpom is the most followed pet on social media, with more than 30 million followers across all channels. He previously held two doggy world records for running the fastest ten meters on his hind legs and for the fastest five meters on his front paws. He also appeared in Katy Perry's "Dark Horse" music video, which has been viewed over three billion times on YouTube.

TIMELINE

50,000 TO 20,000 YEARS AGO
Dogs become the first domesticated animals. It is likely this occurred in multiple places throughout Europe and Asia where their wolf ancestors lived alongside humans.

12,500 YEARS AGO
First archeological evidence of people of the Arctic using dogs to pull sleds.

11,000 TO 10,000 YEARS AGO
People begin domesticating livestock animals with the help of herding dogs.

8,000 TO 9,000 YEARS AGO
Rock art in Saudi Arabia is the earliest example of dogs featured in human art. One petroglyph depicts a hunter with a bow and arrow and thirteen dogs. Two of the dogs are on leashes. Scientists think the leashes could indicate that these two dogs were more valuable or that they were new dogs being trained.

4,000 YEARS AGO
The ancient Mesopotamians were the first society known to include versions of dogs among their gods. Later, Babylonians, Egyptians, Greeks, Mesoamericans, and others included dogs or dog-human hybrids in their mythologies.

2,600 YEARS AGO
One of the earliest accounts of dogs fighting in battle comes from the early kingdom of Lydia in Asia Minor.

1670–1897
A tough breed of mountain rescue dogs, working with monks from the Great Saint Bernard Hospice in Switzerland, saved at least 2,000 people who became lost while traveling through Alpine mountain passes. This breed, now known as St. Bernard, continues to help rescue workers find avalanche victims.

1780
Josef Reisinger, a blind man from Vienna, trained his dog, Spitz, to act as his guide so well that people often questioned whether he was blind. His story was later published in one of the first books to describe methods for training dogs for the blind.

1835
Modern-day dogfighting emerges, pitting dogs against other dogs for sport. This inhumane and illegal practice continues underground today, despite efforts to prevent it.

1859
The first formal dog show in England was held. Just two kinds of dogs were featured: pointers and setters.

1860
An American electrician named James Spratt invented the first commercial dog food after visiting London and watching sailors toss hardtack—a hard, nonperishable biscuit used for sailors' and soldiers' food rations—to dock dogs. Named Fibrine Dog Cakes, the biscuits were one of the most heavily advertised products of the twentieth century.

1866
Henry Bergh founded the American Society for the Prevention of Cruelty to Animals (ASPCA) to raise awareness and advocate for animal abuse legislation. Its original mission was to protect horses, but it expanded to prevent cruelty to dogs in puppy mills and illegal dog fighting, and to come to the aid of dogs during natural disasters. Today the ASPCA helps all animals.

1873
The Kennel Club was established in Britain to officially recognize dog breeds and determine breed standards. French and Italian Kennel Clubs followed in 1882 and the American Kennel Club in 1884.

1899
Dog trainers in Ghent, Belgium, began formally training canines to work alongside law enforcement officers. It was the beginning of the modern police dog, often called a K9, working to help solve crime throughout the world.

1914–1918
Over 50,000 trained military dogs served in the armed forces during WWI.

1919

Greyhound track racing as we know it today began in California. There are still thirty-nine working dog tracks in the United States, even though animal activists are deeply concerned for the welfare of racing dogs.

1925

A deadly diphtheria infection broke out in Nome, Alaska, during a blizzard. Planes and ships couldn't travel, while temperatures dropped below -40°F. But a relay of dog-sledding teams ran five days and nights to deliver an antibody serum in time to stop an epidemic. Many dogs lost their lives saving people.

1939–1945

The role of military dogs expanded during WWII. Highly trained scent dogs were deployed to detect explosives. To this day, no man-made equipment can replace the keen ability of a dog's nose for this dangerous work.

1960

The first trained therapy dogs began assisting people with depression and other psychological health issues.

2020–TODAY

Scent dogs in Finland, Thailand, and elsewhere screened airline passengers for COVID-19 infection during the global pandemic. Studies show dogs can be as effective as conventional rapid testing methods. Around the world, scientists continue to study how COVID-sniffing dogs can be helpful in crowded areas where canines can screen hundreds of people per hour. It should be noted that dogs can be infected by humans with the virus, but fortunately most dogs experience only mild symptoms. Serious cases of COVID-19 among dogs are rare.

SELECTED SOURCES

Bergström, Anders, et al. "Origins and Genetic Legacy of Prehistoric Dogs." *Science*, vol. 370, no. 6516, 2020, pp. 557–64, doi:10.1126/science.aba9572.

Coren, Stanley. *The Pawprints of History: Dogs and the Course of Human Events.* New York: Atria Books, 2003.

Derr, Mark. *How the Dog Became the Dog: From Wolves to Our Best Friends.* New York: Overlook Press, 2011.

——. Phone interview with author, July 23, 2021.

Donnelly, Christina. "The 16 Best Dog Instagrams to Follow Right Now." *Spruce Pets*, www.thesprucepets.com/the-best-dog-instagrams-4165921.

Grimm, David. "Oldest Images of Dogs Show Hunting, Leashes." *Science*, vol. 358, no. 6365, 2017, p. 854, doi:10.1126/science.358.6365.854.

Hare, Brian, and Vanessa Woods. *The Genius of Dogs: Discovering the Unique Intelligence of Man's Best Friend.* New York: Penguin, 2013.

Miklósi Adam. *The Dog: A Natural History.* Princeton, NJ: Princeton University Press, 2018.

Reisner, George A. "The Dog Which was Honored by the King of Upper and Lower Egypt." Bulletin of the Museum of Fine Arts, Boston, 34, No. 206 (December 1936), pp. 96–99.

Sinding, Mikkel-Holger S., et al. "Arctic-Adapted Dogs Emerged at the Pleistocene–Holocene Transition." *Science*, vol. 368, no. 6498, 2020, pp. 1495–99, doi:10.1126/science.aaz8599.